This Book Belongs To

_____

Visit Us at
ChooseJoyPress.com
Sign up for our newsletter
& grab a free gift

How to Verse Map

Verse Mapping helps you dig deeper into your daily scripture reading. It's simple to apply with these steps...

1. **Choose Your Verse** – Use the suggested list at the back or choose a verse you've been wanting to explore. Pick one from your favorite bible translations.

2. **Write Out the Verse** – However you want, print, simple script or as fancy as you want. Highlight or mark up any words you don't understand.

3. **Research the Words** – There are a number of online bible dictionaries to use.

4. **Add Historical Context** – Dig deeper by understand who spoke these words, when and where. Again there are a number of online sources.

5. **Define the Central Idea** – You'll want to re-read the verse (maybe several time) with the new information you've found. Then add the central idea that you understand this verse to mean.

6. **Rewrite the Verse** – But now write it in own words. This is probably the important step and how you will understand and keep this verse in your heart.

7. **Apply the Idea** – Write how you have or you can apply this verse t your life.

8. **Write a Prayer** – Now that you understand this verse, write a pray for yourself.

The Verse I Will Map Today

1 Choose a verse from your favorite bible translation

_____   _____
(Book)   (Date)

_____   _____
(Chapter)   (Verse)

2

Write the Verse (highlight/mark words you don't understand)

3

Research Words (lookup & define words/terms)

Who, When, Where (historical information I've found)

My Prayer (based on this verse)

Apply (how will you use this verse in your life)   8

7   Rewrite the Verse (in your own words)

Central Idea (as you see it)   6

The Verse
I Will
Map Today

1 Choose a verse from your favorite bible translation

_____ _____
(Book)   (Date)

_____ _____
(Chapter)   (Verse)

2

Write the Verse (highlight/mark words you don't understand)

3

Research Words (lookup & define words/terms)

4

Who, When, Where (historical information I've found)

5

My Prayer (based on this verse)

Apply (how will you use this verse in your life) **8**

7 Rewrite the Verse (in your own words)

Central Idea (as you see it) **6**

The Verse
I Will
Map Today

 Choose a verse from your favorite bible translation

_____   _____
(Book)   (Date)

_____   _____
(Chapter)   (Verse)

Write the Verse (highlight/mark words you don't understand)

Research Words (lookup & define words/terms)

Who, When, Where (historical information I've found)

My Prayer (based on this verse)

Apply (how will you use this verse in your life)

Rewrite the Verse (in your own words)

Central Idea (as you see it)

The Verse
I Will
Map Today

Choose a verse from your favorite bible translation

_____   _____
(Book)   (Date)

_____   _____
(Chapter)   (Verse)

Write the Verse (highlight/mark words you don't understand)

Research Words (lookup & define words/terms)

Who, When, Where (historical information I've found)

My Prayer (based on this verse)

Apply (how will you use this verse in your life)

Rewrite the Verse (in your own words)

Central Idea (as you see it)

The Verse
I Will
Map Today

 Choose a verse from your favorite bible translation

_____   _____
(Book)   (Date)

_____   _____
(Chapter)   (Verse)

Write the Verse (highlight/mark words you don't understand)

Research Words (lookup & define words/terms)

Who, When, Where (historical information I've found)

My Prayer (based on this verse)

Apply (how will you use this verse in your life) 8

7 Rewrite the Verse (in your own words)

Central Idea (as you see it) 6

The Verse
I Will
Map Today

Choose a verse from your
favorite bible translation

_____   _____
(Book)   (Date)

_____   _____
(Chapter)   (Verse)

Write the Verse (highlight/mark words you don't understand)

Research Words (lookup & define words/terms)

Who, When, Where (historical information I've found)

My Prayer (based on this verse)

Apply (how will you use this verse in your life)

 Rewrite the Verse (in your own words)

Central Idea (as you see it) 6

The Verse
I Will
Map Today

1 Choose a verse from your favorite bible translation

_____   _____
(Book)   (Date)

_____   _____
(Chapter)   (Verse)

2

Write the Verse (highlight/mark words you don't understand)

3

Research Words (lookup & define words/terms)

4

Who, When, Where (historical information I've found)

5

My Prayer (based on this verse)

Apply (how will you use this verse in your life) 8

7 Rewrite the Verse (in your own words)

Central Idea (as you see it) 6

The Verse I Will Map Today

 ① Choose a verse from your favorite bible translation

_____ _____
(Book)   (Date)

_____ _____
(Chapter)   (Verse)

②

Write the Verse (highlight/mark words you don't understand)

③

 Research Words (lookup & define words/terms)

④

Who, When, Where (historical information I've found)

 ⑤

My Prayer (based on this verse)

Apply (how will you use this verse in your life)

Rewrite the Verse (in your own words)

Central Idea (as you see it)

The Verse
I Will
Map Today

 Choose a verse from your favorite bible translation

_____   _____
(Book)   (Date)

_____   _____
(Chapter)   (Verse)

Write the Verse (highlight/mark words you don't understand)

Research Words (lookup & define words/terms)

Who, When, Where (historical information I've found)

My Prayer (based on this verse)

Apply (how will you use this verse in your life)

 Rewrite the Verse (in your own words)

Central Idea (as you see it) 6

The Verse
I Will
Map Today

 Choose a verse from your favorite bible translation

_____   _____
(Book)   (Date)

_____   _____
(Chapter)   (Verse)

Write the Verse (highlight/mark words you don't understand)

Research Words (lookup & define words/terms)

Who, When, Where (historical information I've found)

My Prayer (based on this verse)

Apply (how will you use this verse in your life) **8**

7 Rewrite the Verse (in your own words)

Central Idea (as you see it) **6**

The Verse
I Will
Map Today

 Choose a verse from your
favorite bible translation

_____   _____
(Book)   (Date)

_____   _____
(Chapter)   (Verse)

Write the Verse (highlight/mark words you don't understand)

Research Words (lookup & define words/terms)

Who, When, Where (historical information I've found)

My Prayer (based on this verse)

Apply (how will you use this verse in your life)

Rewrite the Verse (in your own words)

Central Idea (as you see it)

The Verse
I Will
Map Today

 ① Choose a verse from your favorite bible translation

_____   _____
(Book)   (Date)

_____   _____
(Chapter)   (Verse)

②

Write the Verse (highlight/mark words you don't understand)

③

Research Words (lookup & define words/terms)

 ④

Who, When, Where (historical information I've found)

⑤

My Prayer (based on this verse)

Apply (how will you use this verse in your life)

Rewrite the Verse (in your own words)

Central Idea (as you see it)

The Verse
I Will
Map Today

 Choose a verse from your favorite bible translation

_____ _____
(Book)   (Date)

_____ _____
(Chapter)   (Verse)

Write the Verse (highlight/mark words you don't understand)

Research Words (lookup & define words/terms)

Who, When, Where (historical information I've found)

My Prayer (based on this verse)

Apply (how will you use this verse in your life) 8

7 Rewrite the Verse (in your own words)

Central Idea (as you see it) 6

The Verse
I Will
Map Today

 Choose a verse from your favorite bible translation

_____ _____
(Book)   (Date)

_____ _____
(Chapter)   (Verse)

Write the Verse (highlight/mark words you don't understand)

Research Words (lookup & define words/terms)

Who, When, Where (historical information I've found)

My Prayer (based on this verse)

Apply (how will you use this verse in your life)

 Rewrite the Verse (in your own words)

Central Idea (as you see it)

The Verse I Will Map Today

 ① Choose a verse from your favorite bible translation

_____ _____
(Book)   (Date)

_____ _____
(Chapter)   (Verse)

Write the Verse (highlight/mark words you don't understand)

③

Research Words (lookup & define words/terms)

④

Who, When, Where (historical information I've found)

⑤

My Prayer (based on this verse)

Apply (how will you use this verse in your life)

 Rewrite the Verse (in your own words)

Central Idea (as you see it)

The Verse
I Will
Map Today

1 Choose a verse from your favorite bible translation

_____   _____
(Book)   (Date)

_____   _____
(Chapter)   (Verse)

2

Write the Verse (highlight/mark words you don't understand)

3

Research Words (lookup & define words/terms)

4

Who, When, Where (historical information I've found)

5

My Prayer (based on this verse)

Apply (how will you use this verse in your life)

Rewrite the Verse (in your own words)

Central Idea (as you see it)

The Verse
I Will
Map Today

_____   _____
(Book)   (Date)

_____   _____
(Chapter)   (Verse)

Write the Verse (highlight/mark words you don't understand)

Research Words (lookup & define words/terms)

Who, When, Where (historical information I've found)

My Prayer (based on this verse)

Apply (how will you use this verse in your life) 8

7 Rewrite the Verse (in your own words)

Central Idea (as you see it) 6

The Verse
I Will
Map Today

 ① Choose a verse from your favorite bible translation

_____   _____
(Book)   (Date)

_____   _____
(Chapter)   (Verse)

②

Write the Verse (highlight/mark words you don't understand)

③

Research Words (lookup & define words/terms)

 ④

Who, When, Where (historical information I've found)

 ⑤

My Prayer (based on this verse)

Apply (how will you use this verse in your life)

 Rewrite the Verse (in your own words)

Central Idea (as you see it) 6

The Verse
I Will
Map Today

1 Choose a verse from your favorite bible translation

_____   _____
(Book)   (Date)

_____   _____
(Chapter)   (Verse)

2

Write the Verse (highlight/mark words you don't understand)

3

Research Words (lookup & define words/terms)

4

Who, When, Where (historical information I've found)

5

My Prayer (based on this verse)

Apply (how will you use this verse in your life) 8

 7 Rewrite the Verse (in your own words)

Central Idea (as you see it) 6

The Verse
I Will
Map Today

 Choose a verse from your favorite bible translation

_____   _____
(Book)   (Date)

_____   _____
(Chapter)   (Verse)

2

Write the Verse (highlight/mark words you don't understand)

3

Research Words (lookup & define words/terms)

4

Who, When, Where (historical information I've found)

5

My Prayer (based on this verse)

Apply (how will you use this verse in your life)   8

7   Rewrite the Verse (in your own words)

Central Idea (as you see it)   6

The Verse I Will Map Today

 Choose a verse from your favorite bible translation

_____ _____
(Book)   (Date)

_____ _____
(Chapter)   (Verse)

Write the Verse (highlight/mark words you don't understand)

Research Words (lookup & define words/terms)

Who, When, Where (historical information I've found)

My Prayer (based on this verse)

Apply (how will you use this verse in your life)

Rewrite the Verse (in your own words)

Central Idea (as you see it)

The Verse I Will Map Today

1 Choose a verse from your favorite bible translation

_____   _____
(Book)   (Date)

_____   _____
(Chapter)   (Verse)

2

Write the Verse (highlight/mark words you don't understand)

3

Research Words (lookup & define words/terms)

4

Who, When, Where (historical information I've found)

5

My Prayer (based on this verse)

Apply (how will you use this verse in your life) 8

Rewrite the Verse (in your own words) 7

Central Idea (as you see it) 6

The Verse
I Will
Map Today

 Choose a verse from your
favorite bible translation

_____   _____
(Book)   (Date)

_____   _____
(Chapter)   (Verse)

Write the Verse (highlight/mark words you don't understand)

Research Words (lookup & define words/terms)

Who, When, Where (historical information I've found)

My Prayer (based on this verse)

Apply (how will you use this verse in your life)

Rewrite the Verse (in your own words)

Central Idea (as you see it)

The Verse
I Will
Map Today

 Choose a verse from your favorite bible translation

_____ _____
(Book)   (Date)

_____ _____
(Chapter)   (Verse)

Write the Verse (highlight/mark words you don't understand)

Research Words (lookup & define words/terms)

Who, When, Where (historical information I've found)

My Prayer (based on this verse)

Apply (how will you use this verse in your life)

 Rewrite the Verse (in your own words)

Central Idea (as you see it)

The Verse
I Will
Map Today

1 Choose a verse from your favorite bible translation

_____   _____
(Book)   (Date)

_____   _____
(Chapter)   (Verse)

2

Write the Verse (highlight/mark words you don't understand)

3

Research Words (lookup & define words/terms)

4

Who, When, Where (historical information I've found)

5

My Prayer (based on this verse)

Apply (how will you use this verse in your life) **8**

7 Rewrite the Verse (in your own words)

Central Idea (as you see it) **6**

The Verse
I Will
Map Today

 Choose a verse from your favorite bible translation

_____   _____
(Book)   (Date)

_____   _____
(Chapter)   (Verse)

Write the Verse (highlight/mark words you don't understand)

Research Words (lookup & define words/terms)

Who, When, Where (historical information I've found)

My Prayer (based on this verse)

Apply (how will you use this verse in your life) 8

Rewrite the Verse (in your own words) 7

Central Idea (as you see it) 6

The Verse I Will Map Today

 1 Choose a verse from your favorite bible translation

_____   _____
(Book)   (Date)

_____   _____
(Chapter)   (Verse)

2

Write the Verse (highlight/mark words you don't understand)

3

Research Words (lookup & define words/terms)

 4

Who, When, Where (historical information I've found)

 5

My Prayer (based on this verse)

Apply (how will you use this verse in your life)   **8**

Rewrite the Verse (in your own words)

7

Central Idea (as you see it)   **6**

The Verse I Will Map Today

 1 Choose a verse from your favorite bible translation

_____ _____
(Book) (Date)

_____ _____
(Chapter) (Verse)

2

Write the Verse (highlight/mark words you don't understand)

3

Research Words (lookup & define words/terms)

 4

Who, When, Where (historical information I've found)

 5

My Prayer (based on this verse)

Apply (how will you use this verse in your life) 8

Rewrite the Verse (in your own words) 7

Central Idea (as you see it) 6

The Verse
I Will
Map Today

 1 Choose a verse from your favorite bible translation

_____ _____
(Book)   (Date)

_____ _____
(Chapter)   (Verse)

2

Write the Verse (highlight/mark words you don't understand)

3

Research Words (lookup & define words/terms)

 4

Who, When, Where (historical information I've found)

 5

My Prayer (based on this verse)

Apply (how will you use this verse in your life)   8

Rewrite the Verse (in your own words)

7

Central Idea (as you see it)   6

The Verse
I Will
Map Today

1 Choose a verse from your favorite bible translation

_____   _____
(Book)   (Date)

_____   _____
(Chapter)   (Verse)

2

Write the Verse (highlight/mark words you don't understand)

3

Research Words (lookup & define words/terms)

4

Who, When, Where (historical information I've found)

5

My Prayer (based on this verse)

Apply (how will you use this verse in your life)

 Rewrite the Verse (in your own words)

Central Idea (as you see it)

The Verse I Will Map Today

1 Choose a verse from your favorite bible translation

_____   _____
(Book)   (Date)

_____   _____
(Chapter)   (Verse)

2

Write the Verse (highlight/mark words you don't understand)

3

Research Words (lookup & define words/terms)

4

Who, When, Where (historical information I've found)

5

My Prayer (based on this verse)

Apply (how will you use this verse in your life)

 Rewrite the Verse (in your own words)

Central Idea (as you see it)

The Verse I Will Map Today

1 Choose a verse from your favorite bible translation

_____ _____
(Book)   (Date)

_____ _____
(Chapter)   (Verse)

2

Write the Verse (highlight/mark words you don't understand)

3

Research Words (lookup & define words/terms)

4

Who, When, Where (historical information I've found)

5

My Prayer (based on this verse)

Apply (how will you use this verse in your life) 8

7 Rewrite the Verse (in your own words)

Central Idea (as you see it) 6

The Verse
I Will
Map Today

 Choose a verse from your favorite bible translation

_____ _____
(Book)   (Date)

_____ _____
(Chapter)   (Verse)

Write the Verse (highlight/mark words you don't understand)

Research Words (lookup & define words/terms)

Who, When, Where (historical information I've found)

My Prayer (based on this verse)

Apply (how will you use this verse in your life)

 Rewrite the Verse (in your own words)

Central Idea (as you see it) 6

The Verse
I Will
Map Today

1 Choose a verse from your favorite bible translation

_____   _____
(Book)   (Date)

_____   _____
(Chapter)   (Verse)

2

Write the Verse (highlight/mark words you don't understand)

3

Research Words (lookup & define words/terms)

4

Who, When, Where (historical information I've found)

5

My Prayer (based on this verse)

Apply (how will you use this verse in your life)

Rewrite the Verse (in your own words)

Central Idea (as you see it)

The Verse
I Will
Map Today

Choose a verse from your
favorite bible translation

_____   _____
(Book)   (Date)

_____   _____
(Chapter)   (Verse)

Write the Verse (highlight/mark words you don't understand)

Research Words (lookup & define words/terms)

Who, When, Where (historical information I've found)

My Prayer (based on this verse)

Apply (how will you use this verse in your life) 8

7 Rewrite the Verse (in your own words)

Central Idea (as you see it) 6

The Verse
I Will
Map Today

 Choose a verse from your favorite bible translation

_____   _____
(Book)   (Date)

_____   _____
(Chapter)   (Verse)

Write the Verse (highlight/mark words you don't understand)

Research Words (lookup & define words/terms)

Who, When, Where (historical information I've found)

My Prayer (based on this verse)

Apply (how will you use this verse in your life)

 Rewrite the Verse (in your own words)

Central Idea (as you see it)

The Verse
I Will
Map Today

① Choose a verse from your favorite bible translation

_____   _____
(Book)   (Date)

_____   _____
(Chapter)   (Verse)

②

Write the Verse (highlight/mark words you don't understand)

③

Research Words (lookup & define words/terms)

④

Who, When, Where (historical information I've found)

⑤

My Prayer (based on this verse)

Apply (how will you use this verse in your life)

Rewrite the Verse (in your own words)

Central Idea (as you see it)

The Verse
I Will
Map Today

1 Choose a verse from your favorite bible translation

_____   _____
(Book)   (Date)

_____   _____
(Chapter)   (Verse)

2

Write the Verse (highlight/mark words you don't understand)

3

Research Words (lookup & define words/terms)

4

Who, When, Where (historical information I've found)

5

My Prayer (based on this verse)

Apply (how will you use this verse in your life)   8

Rewrite the Verse (in your own words)

7

Central Idea (as you see it)   6

The Verse
I Will
Map Today

1 Choose a verse from your favorite bible translation

_____ . _____
(Book)   (Date)

_____   _____
(Chapter)   (Verse)

Write the Verse (highlight/mark words you don't understand)

Research Words (lookup & define words/terms)

Who, When, Where (historical information I've found)

My Prayer (based on this verse)

Apply (how will you use this verse in your life)

 Rewrite the Verse (in your own words)

Central Idea (as you see it)

The Verse
I Will
Map Today

1 Choose a verse from your favorite bible translation

_____   _____
(Book)   (Date)

_____   _____
(Chapter)   (Verse)

2

Write the Verse (highlight/mark words you don't understand)

3

Research Words (lookup & define words/terms)

4

Who, When, Where (historical information I've found)

5

My Prayer (based on this verse)

Apply (how will you use this verse in your life)

Rewrite the Verse (in your own words)

Central Idea (as you see it)

The Verse I Will Map Today

 Choose a verse from your favorite bible translation

_____ _____
(Book)   (Date)

_____ _____
(Chapter)   (Verse)

Write the Verse (highlight/mark words you don't understand)

Research Words (lookup & define words/terms)

Who, When, Where (historical information I've found)

My Prayer (based on this verse)

Apply (how will you use this verse in your life) 8

Rewrite the Verse (in your own words)

7

Central Idea (as you see it) 6

The Verse I Will Map Today

 Choose a verse from your favorite bible translation

_____ _____
(Book)   (Date)

_____ _____
(Chapter)   (Verse)

Write the Verse (highlight/mark words you don't understand)

Research Words (lookup & define words/terms)

Who, When, Where (historical information I've found)

My Prayer (based on this verse)

Apply (how will you use this verse in your life)

 Rewrite the Verse (in your own words)

Central Idea (as you see it)

The Verse
I Will
Map Today

1 Choose a verse from your favorite bible translation

_____   _____
(Book)   (Date)

_____   _____
(Chapter)   (Verse)

2

Write the Verse (highlight/mark words you don't understand)

3

Research Words (lookup & define words/terms)

4

Who, When, Where (historical information I've found)

5

My Prayer (based on this verse)

Apply (how will you use this verse in your life)   8

Rewrite the Verse (in your own words)

7

Central Idea (as you see it)   6

The Verse
I Will
Map Today

1 Choose a verse from your favorite bible translation

_____   _____
(Book)   (Date)

_____   _____
(Chapter)   (Verse)

2

Write the Verse (highlight/mark words you don't understand)

3

Research Words (lookup & define words/terms)

4

Who, When, Where (historical information I've found)

5

My Prayer (based on this verse)

Apply (how will you use this verse in your life)   8

Rewrite the Verse (in your own words)   7

Central Idea (as you see it)   6

The Verse
I Will
Map Today

 Choose a verse from your favorite bible translation

_____   _____
(Book)   (Date)

_____   _____
(Chapter)   (Verse)

Write the Verse (highlight/mark words you don't understand)

Research Words (lookup & define words/terms)

Who, When, Where (historical information I've found)

My Prayer (based on this verse)

Apply (how will you use this verse in your life) **8**

7 Rewrite the Verse (in your own words)

Central Idea (as you see it) **6**

The Verse I Will Map Today

1 Choose a verse from your favorite bible translation

_____   _____
(Book)   (Date)

_____   _____
(Chapter)   (Verse)

2

Write the Verse (highlight/mark words you don't understand)

3

Research Words (lookup & define words/terms)

4

Who, When, Where (historical information I've found)

5

My Prayer (based on this verse)

Apply (how will you use this verse in your life)

Rewrite the Verse (in your own words)

Central Idea (as you see it)

The Verse
I Will
Map Today

 ① Choose a verse from your favorite bible translation

_____   _____
(Book)   (Date)

_____   _____
(Chapter)   (Verse)

②

Write the Verse (highlight/mark words you don't understand)

③

Research Words (lookup & define words/terms)

④

Who, When, Where (historical information I've found)

⑤

My Prayer (based on this verse)

Apply (how will you use this verse in your life) 8

7 Rewrite the Verse (in your own words)

Central Idea (as you see it) 6

The Verse
I Will
Map Today

Choose a verse from your
favorite bible translation

_____   _____
(Book)   (Date)

_____   _____
(Chapter)   (Verse)

Write the Verse (highlight/mark words you don't understand)

Research Words (lookup & define words/terms)

Who, When, Where (historical information I've found)

My Prayer (based on this verse)

Apply (how will you use this verse in your life)

Rewrite the Verse (in your own words)

Central Idea (as you see it)

The Verse I Will Map Today

① Choose a verse from your favorite bible translation

_____ _____
(Book)   (Date)

_____ _____
(Chapter)   (Verse)

②

Write the Verse (highlight/mark words you don't understand)

③

Research Words (lookup & define words/terms)

④

Who, When, Where (historical information I've found)

⑤

My Prayer (based on this verse)

Apply (how will you use this verse in your life)

 Rewrite the Verse (in your own words)

Central Idea (as you see it)

The Verse
I Will
Map Today

 Choose a verse from your
favorite bible translation

_____   _____
(Book)   (Date)

_____   _____
(Chapter)   (Verse)

Write the Verse (highlight/mark words you don't understand)

Research Words (lookup & define words/terms)

Who, When, Where (historical information I've found)

My Prayer (based on this verse)

Apply (how will you use this verse in your life) **8**

7 Rewrite the Verse (in your own words)

Central Idea (as you see it) **6**

The Verse
I Will
Map Today

 ① Choose a verse from your favorite bible translation

_____   _____
(Book)   (Date)

_____   _____
(Chapter)   (Verse)

② Write the Verse (highlight/mark words you don't understand)

③

Research Words (lookup & define words/terms)

④

Who, When, Where (historical information I've found)

⑤

My Prayer (based on this verse)

Apply (how will you use this verse in your life)

Rewrite the Verse (in your own words)

Central Idea (as you see it)

The Verse
I Will
Map Today

1 Choose a verse from your favorite bible translation

_____   _____
(Book)   (Date)

_____   _____
(Chapter)   (Verse)

2

Write the Verse (highlight/mark words you don't understand)

3

Research Words (lookup & define words/terms)

4

Who, When, Where (historical information I've found)

5

My Prayer (based on this verse)

Apply (how will you use this verse in your life)

 Rewrite the Verse (in your own words)

Central Idea (as you see it)

The Verse
I Will
Map Today

Choose a verse from your
favorite bible translation

_____   _____
(Book)   (Date)

_____   _____
(Chapter)   (Verse)

Write the Verse (highlight/mark words you don't understand)

Research Words (lookup & define words/terms)

Who, When, Where (historical information I've found)

My Prayer (based on this verse)

Apply (how will you use this verse in your life)

Rewrite the Verse (in your own words)

Central Idea (as you see it)

The Verse
I Will
Map Today

 Choose a verse from your favorite bible translation

_____   _____
(Book)   (Date)

_____   _____
(Chapter)   (Verse)

Write the Verse (highlight/mark words you don't understand)

Research Words (lookup & define words/terms)

Who, When, Where (historical information I've found)

My Prayer (based on this verse)

Apply (how will you use this verse in your life)

 Rewrite the Verse (in your own words)

Central Idea (as you see it)

The Verse I Will Map Today

1 Choose a verse from your favorite bible translation

_____   _____
(Book)   (Date)

_____   _____
(Chapter)   (Verse)

2

Write the Verse (highlight/mark words you don't understand)

3

Research Words (lookup & define words/terms)

4

Who, When, Where (historical information I've found)

My Prayer (based on this verse)

Apply (how will you use this verse in your life) 8

 7 Rewrite the Verse (in your own words)

Central Idea (as you see it) 6

The Verse
I Will
Map Today

Choose a verse from your favorite bible translation

_____   _____
(Book)   (Date)

_____   _____
(Chapter)   (Verse)

Write the Verse (highlight/mark words you don't understand)

Research Words (lookup & define words/terms)

Who, When, Where (historical information I've found)

My Prayer (based on this verse)

Apply (how will you use this verse in your life) 8

Rewrite the Verse (in your own words) 7

Central Idea (as you see it) 6

The Verse I Will Map Today

 Choose a verse from your favorite bible translation

_____   _____
(Book)   (Date)

_____   _____
(Chapter)   (Verse)

Write the Verse (highlight/mark words you don't understand)

Research Words (lookup & define words/terms)

Who, When, Where (historical information I've found)

My Prayer (based on this verse)

Apply (how will you use this verse in your life)

Rewrite the Verse (in your own words)

Central Idea (as you see it)

The Verse
I Will
Map Today

1 Choose a verse from your favorite bible translation

_____   _____
(Book)   (Date)

_____   _____
(Chapter)   (Verse)

2

Write the Verse (highlight/mark words you don't understand)

3

Research Words (lookup & define words/terms)

4

Who, When, Where (historical information I've found)

5

My Prayer (based on this verse)

Apply (how will you use this verse in your life) 8

 7 Rewrite the Verse (in your own words)

Central Idea (as you see it) 6

The Verse
I Will
Map Today

 Choose a verse from your favorite bible translation

_____   _____
(Book)   (Date)

_____   _____
(Chapter)   (Verse)

Write the Verse (highlight/mark words you don't understand)

Research Words (lookup & define words/terms)

Who, When, Where (historical information I've found)

My Prayer (based on this verse)

Apply (how will you use this verse in your life)   **8**

7   Rewrite the Verse (in your own words)

Central Idea (as you see it)   **6**

The Verse
I Will
Map Today

① Choose a verse from your favorite bible translation

_____ _____
(Book)   (Date)

_____ _____
(Chapter)   (Verse)

②

Write the Verse (highlight/mark words you don't understand)

③

Research Words (lookup & define words/terms)

④

Who, When, Where (historical information I've found)

⑤

My Prayer (based on this verse)

Apply (how will you use this verse in your life)

8

7

Rewrite the Verse (in your own words)

Central Idea (as you see it)

6

Suggested Verses

Isaiah 57:18-19	2 Thessalonians 3:3	Psalm 91:2
Joshua 1:9	Luke 12:31	Deuteronomy 4:31
Psalm 28:6	2 Chronicles 30:9	2 Corinthians 9:15
Ephesians 1:4-5	Proverbs 19:21	Daniel 2:21
Job 12:13	Psalm 115:12-13	Isaiah 26:1
Acts 4:12	Revelation 7:17	2 Timothy 3:16
Psalm 119:105	Zephaniah 3:17	2 Peter 1:3
Proverbs 8:35	Job 10:12	Luke 2:14
Nehemiah 8:10	Jeremiah 15:16	John 16:33
Ezekiel 34:15	Psalm 103:8	Romans 1:17
Matthew 28:20	Acts 2:25	Philippians 1:6
Proverbs 3:3-4	Isaiah 26:3	Romans 8:6
Titus 2:11	Acts 15:11	1 Corinthians 15:10
Psalm 25:3	Proverbs 3:5-6	Ephesians 6:18
Matthew 21:22	Isaiah 51:12	Daniel 9:9
Malachi 3:10	1 Thessalonians 5:18	Jeremiah 10:23
Psalm 31:14-15	John 14:27	Ephesians 4:7
2 Corinthians 5:7	Mark 9:23	Psalm 105:3

Bible Mapping Resources

(collect your own online and offline resources and
add them her for easy reference)

Resource	Type	Location
_____	_____	_____
_____	_____	_____
_____	_____	_____
_____	_____	_____
_____	_____	_____
_____	_____	_____
_____	_____	_____
_____	_____	_____
_____	_____	_____
_____	_____	_____
_____	_____	_____
_____	_____	_____
_____	_____	_____
_____	_____	_____
_____	_____	_____
_____	_____	_____
_____	_____	_____
_____	_____	_____
_____	_____	_____

More From

GOD, Coffee & Me
Build a stronger relationship with God every morning with this prayer journal with scripture.
Type the ISBN#
1718057954
Into search
(Amazon or Google)

Take the Scripture Writing Challenge
Dig deeper into the topic of Joy and get creative with your bible study.
Type the ISBN#
1731009887
Into search
(Amazon or Google)

CPSIA information can be obtained
at www.ICGtesting.com
Printed in the USA
LVHW081527020519
616408LV00028B/745/P